and and and and
and and and and

Abdul

Adn
Sentence making   07/Dec/2020

A dog has four legs.
A dog has four legs.
d   d   d   d   d
d d d d d d d
d d d dogg duck

Adn has done reading
and writing today.   duck

Small
Less than 6

Number line from 0 to 8 with a point marked at 4.

13/Jan/2021

a b c d

a b c d

a b c d

a b c d

one two three ☆

one two three

one two three

e f g h i k

e f g h i k k

ea

cream feast

heap jean

seal sea

beach beans

seat team

IPB

Printed in Great Britain
by Amazon